Poetic Philosophy Presents

Narrative Translations Designed for Accessibility

Nietzsche's Thus Also Zarathustra

A Mountain Overture

Translated as Dynamite

By Jason Kassel, PhD

Recursive Publishing

Table of Contents

Translator’s Introduction

This is not your professor’s Nietzsche.

This is Nietzsche on fire.
Not classified, not footnoted, not explained to death.
Not filtered through three centuries of academic timidity.

This is Nietzsche as dynamite.

Not a system. Not a method.
A voice, a rhythm, a mask, a mountain.
A prophet who walks alone,
but never without thunder.

Why A Mountain Overture?

Because Nietzsche's Also sprach Zarathustra begins not as argument but as initiation.
The Vorspiel - often translated “Prelude” - is really an Overture:
a dramatic, prophetic unveiling of all that will follow.
Like an overture in music, it foreshadows every theme to come:
solitude, descent, death, laughter, flame, return.

It begins on the mountain -
and returns there -
but only after walking through the market, the fall, the

corpse, the laugh.
Zarathustra does not teach from above.
He descends, disappears, dies, returns.

This translation follows him.

Why “Translated as Dynamite”?

Nietzsche warned us:
"I am not a man, I am dynamite."

But he has been handled like porcelain,
sanded down to make him safe for lecture halls.
This version resists that.
No antique politesse. No scholar’s museum-glass. No flattening of metaphors.

Instead:

- Short lines – to preserve his cadence.
- Concrete verbs – to let his will move.
- Metaphor carried through – not abandoned halfway.
- The Overman not explained – but walked with.

- God not footnoted – but dead.

The goal is not to interpret Nietzsche.
The goal is to stand in his weather.

Who Is This For?

For readers who have been handed Nietzsche as a relic.
For those who found Thus Spoke Zarathustra confusing, distant, over-ornamented.
For the student who wants to feel the heat behind the words,
not just the history around them.

This is not your professor's Nietzsche.

This is the one who climbs into the storm,
laughs alone in the dark,
and plants fire in your bones.

Visual Legend: Symbols That Speak Without Words

△ The Mountain

Symbol of: Solitude, Height, Vision, Origin
The starting place. The returning place.
Where Zarathustra goes to see clearly - and to become wide.
Not escape from man, but preparation for descent.

🪢 The Rope

Symbol of: Man, Tension, Risk, Becoming
Stretched between beast and Overman.
Man is not a goal, but a tightrope -
a bridge between past and future, meaning and abyss.

☀ The Sun

Symbol of: Creative Force, Life-Affirmation, Overman
Zarathustra's silent companion.
Burns without apology.
Shines not to command, but to awaken.

∇ The Abyss

Symbol of: Truth, Fear, Eternal Return

That which opens when we look too deeply.

Nietzsche's great mirror.

He who can laugh into the abyss - creates.

🜃 The Flame

Symbol of: Spirit, Will, Transformation

The soul that dances.

What does not burn remains untested.

Zarathustra speaks not to inform, but to ignite.

🜁 The Wind

Symbol of: Movement, Voice, Isolation

Zarathustra often speaks to the wind.

His words scatter, unreceived - until they root in the ready.

Truth moves like weather, not like law.

🐍 The Serpent

Symbol of: Wisdom, Time, Eternal Return
Wound around the sun. Partner to the eagle.
Does not preach. Does not serve.
It coils and returns - like truth.

🦅 The Eagle

Symbol of: Strength, Sovereignty, Silence
Sees far. Flies alone.
Not a master - but a creature of high air.
Zarathustra's companion in solitude.

🎭 The Mask

Symbol of: Role, Distance, Metaphor
Zarathustra is both man and myth.
Nietzsche is both author and actor.
Only through the mask can truth sometimes speak.

● The Shadow

Symbol of: Past Self, Doubt, Echo
Grows longer as Zarathustra climbs.
He must learn not to flee it - but to speak with it.
The shadow follows - not to haunt, but to remind.

Prologue - Overture on the Mountains

§1 – Opening Scene

When Zarathustra was thirty years old,
he left his homeland -
and the mirror-lake of his homeland -
and went up into the mountain.

There he enjoyed the company of his spirit
and the depth of his solitude,
and for ten years,
he did not grow tired of either.

---

§2 – The Descent Begins

But at last,
his heart underwent a metamorphosis.

One morning, with the dawnlight,
he rose -
stepped before the sun -
and spoke to it like this:

"You great star!
What would your joy be,
if not for those you shine upon?

For ten years,
you have climbed up to my cave:
without me -
without my eagle,
and my serpent -
you might have grown weary
of your light
and of this path."

---

§3 – The Decision to Go Down

At that, Zarathustra left his cave,
like a dancer,
light of foot and firm of will.

For many dawns,
he had walked toward the valley below,
meeting no one.

But when he came to the forest's edge -
suddenly there stood before him
an old man
who had left his holy hut
to gather roots in the woods.

And the old man spoke:

“No stranger walks in my mountain!
What brings the changed Zarathustra here?
Once you stayed proud and still in your cave -
did you not eat your food in the forest,
and drink from your spring
like a beast?”

Zarathustra answered:

“I love mankind.”

“Why,” said the old man, “did I go into the forest and wilderness?
Was it not because I loved humans too much?

Now I love God,
and not men.
Man is for me too imperfect a thing.
Love for man would kill me.”

Zarathustra replied:

“What did I say of love?
I bring a gift!”

“Do not go to mankind,” said the old man.
“Stay in the forest.
Go back to the animals.
Why not be like me -
a god who lives without men?”

But Zarathustra went on his way,
thinking only:

Could it be?
This old saint in the forest
has not yet heard
that God is dead?

---

§4 – The Descent to the Market

When Zarathustra reached the nearest town,
he found many people gathered in the square -
for it had been announced
that a tightrope-walker would perform.

And Zarathustra spoke to the crowd:

“I teach you the Overman.
Man is something that must be overcome.
What have you done to overcome him?

All creatures so far
created something beyond themselves -
and do you want to be the ebb of this great
tide,
and not the wave that breaks beyond it?

What is the ape to man?
A laughingstock,
or a painful embarrassment.
Just so shall man be to the Overman:
a laughingstock,
or a painful embarrassment.

You have made your way
from worm to man -
and much in you
is still worm.

Once you were apes,
and still today man is more ape than any ape.

Even the wisest among you
is only a discord and a hybrid
of plant and ghost.

But do I command you
to become ghosts or plants?

Behold, I teach you the Overman!

The Overman is the meaning of the earth.
Let your will say:
the Overman shall be
the meaning of the earth!

I ask you, my brothers, remain faithful to the earth -
and do not believe those who speak to you
of otherworldly hopes!

They are poisoners -
whether they know it or not.

They are despisers of life,
the dying and decaying,
of whom the earth is weary.

So let them be gone!"

---

§5 – The Tightrope-Walker

Zarathustra saw the people laughing.
The tightrope-walker had begun his act.
He stepped out from a high tower,
walking above the crowd on a rope stretched between two rooftops.

But Zarathustra continued speaking:

"Man is a rope,
stretched between animal and Overman -
a rope over an abyss.

A dangerous crossing.
A dangerous on-the-way.
A dangerous looking-back.
A dangerous shuddering and standing-still.

What is great in man
is that he is a bridge,
and not an end.

What can be loved in man
is that he is an overture
and a going-under.

I love those who do not know how to live,
except by going under -
for they are the ones who cross over."

---

§6 – The Fall

But when Zarathustra had spoken these words,
someone called out from the crowd:
"We've heard enough of the tightrope-walker - now let's see him!"

And all the people laughed at Zarathustra.
But the tightrope-walker, believing the words applied to him,
stepped onto the rope.

He had gone only a few steps
when a figure leapt out from the tower behind him -
a jester in motley clothes, agile and light.

"Out of the way, you slowpoke!" cried the jester,
and he sprang over the tightrope-walker.

The walker was startled, lost his balance -
and fell.

His arms flailed.
He twisted through the air like a flame snuffed out by the wind.
He crashed to the ground like a broken puppet.

The crowd rushed toward the fallen man -
but Zarathustra stood at his side.

At last, the man opened his eyes.
Zarathustra knelt beside him.

"What are you doing here?" the man asked.
"I knew long ago I would fall.
Not from my art -
but from lack of meaning.
I was not more than a metaphor."

Zarathustra answered:

“You have made danger your calling.
There is nothing shameful in your fall.”

The dying man whispered:

“I knew I would fall.
But now - I die not alone.”

---

§7 – The Burial of the Rope-Walker

At sunset, Zarathustra carried the dead man on his back
and left the town.

He had not yet gone far
when he met a man on the road - a gravedigger.

The gravedigger looked at the burden Zarathustra carried
and said, “You are carrying your corpse out of town?”

Zarathustra answered,
“Yes. It is my companion. I honor what fell.”

“You’re carrying your dead man far,” said the gravedigger.
“But Zarathustra has no home.
So where will you bury him?”

Zarathustra replied:
"Whoever gives his life for his truth,
I will make a resting place for him."

He brought the body to a hollow tree in the forest.
There he laid him to rest, wrapped in clean cloth.

Then he spoke to the corpse:

> "I buried you with my own hands -
> and your death became a tie that binds me to mankind.
>
> I shall carry your death as a seed within me.
> You were a symbol -
> and I will honor what you meant.
>
> The tightrope is still stretched between beast and Overman -
> and I will not leave until I have walked it."

---

§8 – The Sleepless Night and the Laugh

At midnight, Zarathustra rose from his bed.
He looked into the dark forest
and spoke to his heart:

> "A light has gone out in me -
> I must be a new flame.

My first gift to mankind
was a corpse.

I give, but they do not understand.
They laugh at me.

They do not hear the voice of the giver."

Then Zarathustra wept.
But not for long.

He wiped his tears
and laughed.

And he said:

"To weep and to laugh
are of the same root.
We break open the shell of our darkness
in both ways.

I will make my gift anew.
I will not return to the forest.
The path goes forward -
even if no one follows."

And he stepped into the night
with a new strength in his gait.

---

§§9–10 – The Second Descent and the Call to the Givers

In the morning, Zarathustra returned to the town.
He stood again before the people
and spoke these words:

"I am not for all.
I am for those who hear me.

You mock me.
You do not know the weight of my gifts.

You are not yet ready
for the flame
that does not consume
but gives.

Behold, I seek the creators -
the harvesters -
the sowers of seed.

I seek those who write new values
on new tablets.

I seek those who build
beyond their own time.

The lightning sleeps
in the root of their being.

They laugh not to mock -
but to conquer.

They are not afraid to go under,
for they have seen the summit."

Then Zarathustra left the crowd.
No one followed.

He went alone,
but his steps were steady.

He said to himself:

"The time is not yet ripe.

My harvest is not for these shallow valleys.

I go to the mountains -
to wait for those
who are heavy with lightning
and hungry for earth."

And so he vanished into solitude once more -
not in sorrow,
but in readiness.

Book I

Discourse 1 - On the Three Metamorphoses

Zarathustra spoke:

"I will tell you of three metamorphoses
of the spirit:
how it becomes a camel,
then a lion,
and finally a child.

The spirit longs for burden.
It wants to kneel,
to carry weight.
Like the camel,
it seeks the heaviest load.

It asks:
'Who will command me to bow low?
Who will burden me that I may rejoice
in bearing it?'

And so the camel kneels -
and takes upon itself
the burden of knowledge,
of duty,
of sacrifice.

But in the loneliest desert,
the second transformation comes:
the spirit becomes a lion.

It wants to conquer its freedom
and be lord in its own wilderness.

It seeks out its final master -
and its final god -
and it says to him:
'You shall not command me!'

But to create new freedom
is not enough:
the lion cannot create new values.
It must win the right
to create.

And so, at last, the child is born.

Innocence.
Forgetfulness.
A sacred Yes.

The child is the beginning.
A fresh wheel.
A self-turning sun.
A first step.
A holy play."

Zarathustra fell silent.
And the people marveled -
but they did not understand.

Discourse 2 - On the Chairs of Virtue

Zarathustra went into a town where many teachers of virtue sat.
They were praised by the people
and honored with golden chairs.

Zarathustra listened as one spoke:

> "You shall obey.
> You shall do your duty.
> You shall honor father and mother,
> and do good to your neighbor.
>
> Virtue is obedience.
> Virtue is order.
> Virtue is following the law."

Zarathustra laughed.

Then he spoke:

> "You speak of taming.
> You speak of habits dressed in praise.

But tell me -
have you ever heard a song rise
from obedience?

You call it virtue -
but I see only chains
hidden in flowers.

A dog that sits when told -
is that your highest man?

I say:
the noble spirit does not obey.
It creates its own law.

The noble spirit walks like the wind -
dancing where the chairs are nailed down.

And when it gives,
it gives not to be thanked -
but because giving overflows from it.

You teach virtue as quiet servitude.
I teach it as fire that gives warmth -
and consumes."

And the people looked at Zarathustra with unease.
Some laughed.
Some scowled.
But none followed.

Discourse 3 - Von den Hinterweltlern

Zarathustra spoke to the people:

"Once, the soul looked upon the body
and thought: this is suffering.

And it wished to escape.

So the soul invented other worlds -
invisible ones,
better ones,
where it would no longer need to feel.

Thus were born
the heavens,
the beyonds,
the gods of comfort.

They are the dreams
of the weary body,
the poisoned heart,
the hurt flesh that could not bear its own
shadow.

But I say:
there is no world behind this one.

There is only this earth -
and the body that sings upon it.

The body is a great reason -
a dance of senses and strength.
The soul is just a word
for something about the body.

You say:
'Our spirit is trapped in flesh!'
But I say:
'Your spirit is too thin -
it cannot carry the body's depth.'

You flee to the heavens
because you cannot yet stand on the earth.

You call me a blasphemer.
But I ask you:
which is more sacred -
the wound,
or the healing?

Which is more holy -
a dream of flight,
or the will that walks?"

Then Zarathustra turned from them,
and his shadow fell long on the stones.

Discourse 4 - On the Despisers of the Body

Zarathustra spoke:

“To you I speak,
you despisers of the body -
you are not bridges,
you are endings.

You think yourselves pure.
But your body is sick -
and you would rather escape
than be healed.

Your soul is vanity.
A mirror that does not reflect.
A player that does not play.

You say:
‘The body is a chain; it enslaves me.’
But you lie -
it is your weakness that cannot carry the
strength of the body.

You say:
‘The body is a tool; the soul commands.’
But I say:

your soul is just a word
for what happens in the body.

A great reason lives in every limb,
every pulse and desire.
The body does not lie -
it sings what it needs.

The body is your teacher,
your war,
your home.

You call yourself superior?
You look down on the ground where you walk?

I tell you:
the earth does not need your contempt.
It needs your dance.

Let your spirit become body,
let your body become spirit -
and let both become joy."

Then Zarathustra turned his back
on those who sat pale with piety,
and his voice no longer reached them.

Discourse 5 - On Joys and Passions

Zarathustra spoke:

"My brothers,
do not trust those who speak of passions with fear.
They say: passions are wild beasts -
bind them, silence them, chain them.

But I say:
your passions are not beasts,
they are roots.
They grow toward the sun
if you do not rot them in the dark.

What is called sin
is often only misunderstood hunger.

What is called virtue
is often only tamed fear.

Do not break your passions -
transform them.

Do not dig them up -
cultivate them.

Joys are not the enemy of the spirit.
They are its music.

And the strongest joys
have always sprung from passions
that became creative.

Lust that becomes rhythm.
Rage that becomes power.
Grief that becomes depth.
Hunger that becomes gift.

The soul grows not by denial -
but by overflowing.

I do not teach repression.
I teach fermentation."

And the people whispered to one another:
"He speaks like wine,
but we are not thirsty."

Discourse 6 - On the Pale Criminal

Zarathustra spoke:

"You do not understand the criminal.
You fear him.
You pity him.
You want to cure him.

But I ask you:
what if his blade was honest -
and his hand trembled only after the strike?

What if his sickness
was not his cruelty,
but his conscience?

There are souls
who cannot bear their heights -
and so they leap
into darkness.

They commit the deed
not out of wickedness,
but out of a failure of unity.

Their hands are stronger than their hearts -
and their hearts accuse them after.

You call them evil.
I call them broken.

You say: 'He should repent!'
But I say:
he must become whole.

The pale criminal does not need your pity.
He needs a new fire -

one that melts the frost
between his will and his soul."

Then Zarathustra turned from the judges,
and looked not at the criminal,
but at the crowd.

"You are paler than he is.
For you have never dared
to strike."

Discourse 7 - On Reading and Writing

Zarathustra spoke:

"Of all writing,
I love only what is written in blood.
Write with blood -
and you will learn
that blood is spirit.

It is not easy to understand me.
And I do not want it to be.

A thing has value
only when it is hard to get.

You read with your fingers,
not your eyes.

You feel the page
but not the wound.

Let writing be a wound.
Let it burn,
let it breathe,
let it bite back.

I do not write for those
who are hungry for words -
but for those who are starving
for meaning.

You ask for short words,
easy truths.
But I say:
only the slow words that grow
in the dark
have roots.

You say:
'This thinker bites!'
But why would you pet a lion?

Let your soul be wild.
Let your words leap.
Let your silence speak."

Then Zarathustra looked into the mountains,
and his voice became quiet.

> "I am not a writer.
> I am a wind.
> A flame.
> A hammer."

Discourse 8 - The Tree on the Mountain

Zarathustra had climbed alone again.
High on the mountain,
he met a young man with troubled eyes.

The youth spoke:

> "I can no longer bear being among men.
> I am torn between shame and disgust.
>
> I long for the purity of heights -
> but I am not yet strong enough to live in solitude."

Zarathustra answered:

> "You are like a tree
> that has grown too close to the ground.

Its roots want to reach deep.
Its branches want to rise -
but the shadow of the crowd keeps it stunted.

You seek your own way,
but the noise of others bends you.

You are not weak -
you are not broken -
you are becoming.

Do not flee from mankind
because you are ashamed of it.
Flee only when you are ready
to return with strength.

You say the heights call you?
Then grow toward them.
But do not forget -
the deeper the roots,
the taller the tree."

The young man sat in silence.
And Zarathustra, too, was quiet -
for he knew the silence was growing.

Discourse 9 - On the Preachers of Death

Zarathustra spoke:

"There are those
who preach retreat from life.

They say:
'Life is suffering.
Life is filth.
Life is error.'

And so they call you to death
as if it were salvation.

But I say:
they are the poisoned -
and they want the world to drink with them.

They do not create.
They do not dance.
They do not laugh.

They call themselves 'saints,'
but they are weary of the earth.

Beware those who whisper:
'You must die to be pure.'
They have already turned away from joy.

Beware those who say:
'Your desires are sinful.'

They cannot bear
the heat of a burning soul.

They are preachers of death.
Even when they speak of virtue -
they smell of the tomb.

I do not hear the breath of life in them.
I hear the rustling of dry leaves
and bones.

I love those
who love to live -
who long for the sunrise
and the thunder,
the seed,
and the storm.

I do not preach death.
I preach becoming."

Then Zarathustra turned his face to the wind,
and it carried his words beyond the ears of the crowd.

Discourse 10 - On War and Warriors

Zarathustra spoke:

"I do not call you to slay,
but to fight.

Not against men,
but against what in you
is cowardly, soft, and herd-like.

Your enemy is not out there -
it is the sleep within you,
the comfort that chokes your fire.

I do not teach you to carry weapons.
I teach you to carry flame.

Let your will be a sword.
Let your knowledge be a bow.
Let your heart be a shield.

You say:
'There is no enemy.'
But I say:
You have not yet seen yourself clearly.

The path to the Overman
is not paved with peace.

It is cut with resistance,
with self-overcoming,
with the courage to stand alone.

I do not want disciples.
I want warriors -
those who risk everything
for the sake of becoming.

Laugh in the face of fear.
Walk where the weak would kneel.
Build in storms.
Burn in solitude.

The hour calls not for sleep,
but for lightning."

And Zarathustra's voice cracked the stillness
like thunder from a high crag.
The people trembled -
but no one moved.

Discourse 11 - On the New Idol

Zarathustra spoke:

"Some bow no longer before old gods.
But they still kneel -
before the new idol.

This idol has skin of iron
and breathes smoke.

It devours your will
and calls it 'law.'

I speak of the state.

Where the people once created -
now the state consumes.

It takes the highest and lowest
and grinds them down to sameness.
It calls this 'equality' -
but it is erasure.

The state wants to be your shepherd.
But it is only a butcher
in a mask of care.

It offers you safety -
in exchange for your soul.

You must obey.
You must serve.
You must forget how to live without it.

But I say:
Flee from the great noise and great numbers.

The state is where all men are poisoners -
where all virtues rot
into bureaucracy.

Where no one dares be great,
because greatness has no office.

There, even the voice of the poet
becomes state-sanctioned music
for the dead.

I love what the state fears:
the solitary,
the creator,
the one who laughs at flags.

Break the idol.
The state is a cold monster -
it bites with the teeth
of the many who are afraid."

And Zarathustra left the place of speeches and crowds,
and returned to his cave
to breathe.

Discourse 12 - On the Flies of the Market-Place

Zarathustra spoke:

"Flee, my friend,
into your solitude.

I see you stung by the flies of the market-place

-

those little men

who buzz around every greatness

with praise and venom alike.

You show them your wound,

and they make it their feast.

You speak,

and they twist your word

to feed their swarm.

They do not hate you.

They need you -

to pull down what they cannot build.

I say:

beware their applause

as much as their stones.

Their buzzing is worse than their bite.

You would walk like a storm,

but they drown you in their windless noise.

You would dance on the mountain,

but they drag you back

into their pit of busy nothing.

Be not like the bell
that rings for every hand.

Speak when your soul overflows -
then go silent.

Laugh when they sting -
for they cannot follow you into silence.

And when you can no longer bear their swarm,
climb again.

Solitude is your strength.
From the heights,
even the flies lose their sound."

Then Zarathustra closed his eyes
and heard only the wind above the square.

Discourse 13 - On Chastity

Zarathustra spoke:

"I walk among people
and I see them speak of chastity
as if it were a virtue.

But many of them are chaste
only because their flesh is withered.

Not from strength -
but from dryness.

They do not burn -
so they praise the cold.

Others are chaste out of fear:
afraid of what love will stir,
afraid of falling,
afraid of fire.

But I say:
let your love be bold -
let your desire speak.
Let it not crawl in shame.

Do not call holy
what is only a kind of death.

There are those
who destroy themselves
through restraint.

And there are those
who are so full of fire,
that love overflows from them
like a gift.

These are the ones
who do not speak of chastity -

for they are too alive
to praise absence.

I love the earth.
And I love the body.
And I say:
do not bury your joy
beneath the altar of fear.

Let your longing become creation,
not repression."

Then Zarathustra turned away
from the pale men with hollow eyes,
and walked toward the sun.

Discourse 14 - On the Friend

Zarathustra spoke:

"You call someone a friend -
but what do you mean?

Do you seek comfort?
A mirror?
A hand that agrees with your own?

I say:
the friend is a question,
not an answer.

The friend is the one
who dares to wound you
when you are false -
and to praise you
when you burn true.

Do not seek your equal.
Seek your height.

Let the friend be your challenge -
your shadow on the mountain,
not your echo in the valley.

Many love out of weakness:
they want someone who will carry their
sadness.
But I say:
let your friend be one
who awakens your strength.

Friendship is not pity.
It is fire meeting fire -
and finding more flame.

You want to be loved?
Learn first to walk alone.

You want to be understood?
Then speak something worthy of being misunderstood.

I love him who makes his friend
a path to the Overman -
not a pillow for the soul."

Then Zarathustra sat down beside a stream,
and watched two hawks circle one another
in silence.

Discourse 15 - On the Thousand and One Goals

Zarathustra spoke:

"A thousand paths have men walked -
and each called his path
the goal of life.

One people praised bravery,
another obedience,
another silence,
another cleverness.

Values were born from need,
from fear,
from desire,
from chance.

But each people believed:
'We have found what is good.'
And they carved it in stone.

But I say:
there is no one goal.
There are a thousand and one.
And none are eternal.

What is a goal?
A star thrown ahead -
for the people to follow,
to serve,
to die for.

And when the need changed,
they threw a new star into the sky.

The good is a story
told by the victors.

You want to find meaning?
Then create.

Let your values be born
not from fear,
but from strength.

The time has come
to write new laws -
not with ink,
but with flame.

Let your goal be your own -
and let your life be the bow
that sends the arrow forward."

Then Zarathustra looked up,
and saw the evening star tremble
over the edge of the mountain.

Discourse 16 - On Love of One's Neighbor

Zarathustra spoke:

"You speak of love for your neighbor.
But do you love yourself?

You run to others
to escape your own shadow.

You serve
so you don’t have to ask
what your soul desires.

You help -
because you cannot bear your own need.

I say:
do not love the neighbor out of weakness.

The call to love your neighbor
has become a cage.
A virtue for those who fear solitude.

Your neighbor is too near.
You cannot see far
when your eyes are always lowered.

Flee to yourself.
Live with yourself.
Become your own companion.

Then - when you have made peace
with your own soul -
go to others
not as a savior,
but as a sun.

I do not say:
'Hate your neighbor.'

I say:
'Let your love come from strength,
not from hunger.'"

And Zarathustra walked past those
who whispered about kindness
but knew nothing of solitude.

Discourse 17 - On the Way of the Creating One

Zarathustra spoke:

"You follow the path of the creator?
Then you walk alone.

You will pass through rejection,
misunderstanding,
silence.

The creating one does not obey.
He does not adapt.
He overflows -
and in that overflow,
he makes a world.

Creation is birth.
And every birth has blood.

You will be hated by those
who keep order.
You will be feared by those
who love comfort.

They will say:
'Why change what works?'
And you must answer with your flame.

You will build with your own bones.
You will burn old truths
to light your way.

The creating one is not a collector.
He is a firestarter.

He does not ask permission.
He does not wait for praise.
He walks ahead of the echo.

The crowd cannot follow -
and still he goes.

Joy is his compass.
Danger is his oath.

I call you to this path -
not because it is safe,
but because it is yours."

And Zarathustra carved a spiral into the stone beside him,
and left without looking back.

Discourse 18 - On Old and New Tablets

Zarathustra spoke:

"You have heard:
'You shall not kill.
You shall not steal.
You shall honor the law.'
These are the old tablets.

They were carved when man still knelt -
when obedience was called virtue,
and fear was mistaken for wisdom.

But I say:
the time has come for new tablets.

Let the creating one carve them
not in stone,
but in soul.

You say: 'We need rules!'
And I ask:
For what kind of man?

The herd needs fences.
The weak need warnings.
But what of the one
who writes his own law
with fire?

I do not destroy the old tablets
out of hatred -
but because they are too small
for what is coming.

Your virtues have become prisons.
Your commandments have become chains.

You do good
not because you choose,
but because you were told to.

Let the new law be born
from the Yes-saying spirit.

Let it grow like a tree -
not imposed from above,
but rooted in the earth.

The Overman does not obey laws.
He gives them.
Not to others -
but to himself.

His life is a tablet
written in breath,
in danger,
in joy."

And Zarathustra took the old commandments
and placed them in the river,
where they sank without sound.

Discourse 19 - On the Gift-Giving Virtue

Zarathustra spoke:

"I walk among people
as a tree that bears fruit -
not to be praised,
but because I am full.

My virtue is not obedience,
not purity,
not restraint.

My virtue gives.
It overflows.
It creates.

You speak of duty -
I speak of joy.

The highest virtue is not learned -
it is lived.

It comes not from commandments,
but from the deep Yes
that rises when the self is whole.

The gift-giving virtue does not ask:
'What is good?'
It asks:
'What can I become?'

It does not keep accounts.
It does not wait for thanks.
It gives
as the sun gives light -
because it must.

To give is to risk.
To give is to wound and to bless.

The herd says:
'Be good, and be safe.'
But the giver says:
'Burn, and be reborn.'

The gift-giving virtue creates the Overman.
Not by rule,
but by rhythm.

Not by caution,
but by flame.

I do not command you to be virtuous.
I call you to be dangerously full."

And Zarathustra stood at the edge of the mountain
as the sun poured itself over the valley below.

He opened his hands -
and let fall the last of his words
like seeds into the wind.

Section 20 - On the Gift-Giving Virtue – Part II

Zarathustra spoke:

"Once you were children,
who loved to carve names in bark and stone.
Now you are men -
who must carve values
into the future.

Let your virtue not be a command,
but a river.

Let it run deep,
not loud.

Do not become preachers.
Become wells
from which others may drink
without knowing your name.

I do not give you virtues -
I give you the fire
that makes virtue possible.

What is good?
That which affirms life.

What is evil?
That which chokes becoming.

You speak of sacrifice -
but you still want to be thanked.

I say:
give so much
that you forget you gave.

Love not the weak
because they flatter your strength.
Love them only
if your strength makes them strong.

You shall not be protectors,
but awakeners.

Let your giving have fangs,
and your love have a flame.

For the gift-giving virtue
is not gentle -
it calls what sleeps
to rise and burn."

And Zarathustra looked at the hands of the people -
how they clenched in fear,
how they opened in hunger -
and he said nothing more.

Section 21 - On the Gift-Giving Virtue – Part III

Zarathustra spoke:

"I go now alone, my friends.
The time has come for me to descend again -
not to speak,
but to give.

I go to those
who are hungry for lightning,
not for explanations.

The forest has heard me long enough.
Now the marketplace shall receive
my silence.

I do not seek followers.
I seek sowers.

The earth is ripe.
But it will not bloom
until men bleed for their own becoming.

I love him
whose soul is deep as a wound -
not because he suffers,
but because he dares to heal
with fire.

I love him
who laughs in solitude
and builds in storm.

I love him
who burns his old virtues
to kindle new stars.

I go now -
not to rest,
but to wait.

I am the seed
that falls before the storm,
not after it.

My path is not finished.
But I leave you this:

Become hard.
Become deep.
Become joy.

Let your virtue not be a law -
but a gift that sings."

Then Zarathustra turned his back
on the last of the listeners,
and walked down from the mountain
into the valley of men.

Section 22 - [Final Epilogue or Closing Gesture]

(Note: In some German editions, Section 22 is an unnumbered or lightly marked epilogue. It is brief, symbolic, and often treated as a closing gesture rather than a full discourse.)

Zarathustra descended from the mountain
alone.

He said no more.
The words were behind him.
The silence was before him.

And as he passed again through the forest,
not even the birds called his name.

Only the wind followed -
and even that,
quietly.

Book II

Section 1 - The Child with the Mirror

Zarathustra had been gone for many days.
Now he returned from the mountains,
and none recognized him.

He passed through the towns like a shadow.
No one knew that lightning had walked among them.

At last, he came to a place by the sea -
and there, in the sand, sat a child
holding a mirror.

Zarathustra stopped and looked at the child.
And the child looked back
without fear.

Then Zarathustra said:

> "You are my beginning.
>
> You hold the mirror I once shattered.
>
> You do not speak of good and evil.
> You play.
>
> In your eyes there is no guilt.
> Only the echo of becoming.

The wise grow tired of their knowledge.
The child grows joy from unknowing.

You are the sacred Yes.

When the spirit has passed through burden,
and through battle,
it becomes a child again -
not to return,
but to begin anew.

Tell me, child with the mirror:
do I still cast a shadow?"

But the child said nothing -
and only turned the mirror toward the sea.

And in its surface,
Zarathustra saw not himself,
but the sun rising.

Section 2 - On the Blissful Islands

Zarathustra spoke:

"The world is full of heavy words,
but here - on these islands -
my words float like laughter on the sea.

I do not speak to the many.
I speak to the few
who still know how to hear
the rhythm of becoming.

Here, joy has not yet been poisoned
by pity,
or weighed down by virtue.

Here, we dance with our thoughts -
not drag them like chains.

I say to you, companions of the morning:
beware the preachers of guilt.

They call themselves the righteous.
But their eyes betray resentment,
and their mouths drip honey
over rotting law.

They call joy selfish.
They call laughter sin.
They worship sacrifice,
but cannot bear the sun.

I say:
let your joy be bold.

Let it blaze,
even when others cover their eyes.

A flame does not ask permission to burn.
The sea does not apologize for rising.

I love the earth
because it does not seek redemption.

I love the body
because it does not lie.

My soul is a sea
and my virtue a wave -
not to cleanse,
but to create.

You ask me what is holy?
This:
to say Yes without fear.

Let the old gods fall.
Let their priests choke on silence.

Here, on the blissful islands,
we build altars
not to what is above,
but to what is to come."

And Zarathustra fell quiet -
as if the wind had said the rest.

Section 3 - On Pity

Zarathustra spoke:

"My friends,
beware those who speak of pity
as if it were a virtue.

Pity is a chain
forged in the soul
by weakness.

You think you help the suffering
when you lower yourself to them -
but often,
you simply fear their pain
entering your joy.

I do not wish to be pitied.
I wish to be overcome.

Let the weak find their strength -
not through your tears,
but through your fire.

Pity does not create.
It pauses.
It kneels.

In pity,
you forget the earth
and chain yourself again to the cross.

Do not weep for those who fall -
call them to rise.

Do not cradle the broken -
show them how to burn again.

There is more danger in pity
than in cruelty,
for cruelty reveals itself,
but pity hides
behind the mask of goodness.

You must learn to love
without kneeling,
and to lift without sinking.

I love those who suffer -
not because they suffer,
but because they still burn.

I do not pour oil into their wounds.
I give them salt -
that they might become sea again."

And Zarathustra turned away from the town,
where the people built monuments to suffering,
and walked back into the wind.

Section 4 - On Priests

Zarathustra spoke:

“Once, the priests were those
who sang with the storm -
who danced on mountaintops
and made the gods tremble.

But now?
They are pale men
who preach sacrifice
with sunken eyes.

They wear black
not because they grieve the world,
but because they fear its color.

They call the earth ‘fallen,’
the body ‘sinful,’
joy ‘temptation.’

They call their hunger holiness.

But I say to you:
these priests do not climb to heaven -
they crawl into tombs
and call the darkness divine.

They bend their knees
not out of awe,
but out of weakness.

And in their pity
they poison the strong.

Their god is a ghost
fed by their guilt.
Their prayers are chains
disguised as wings.

They do not love man.
They want man small -
so they can guide him
like a blind animal.

I saw a priest
whose soul crouched
like a spider behind a cross.

And I said:
'Better a thief who climbs
than a priest who kneels forever.'

I do not hate them -
I have outgrown them.

I go where they cannot follow:
into the sun,
into the storm,
into the great Yes of the earth."

And Zarathustra walked into a grove of trees
where the light broke
not through stained glass,
but through living leaves.

Section 5 - On the Virtuous

Zarathustra spoke:

"You speak of the 'good man.'
But I ask you:
good for what?

You praise those who obey.
You lift up those who follow rules.
But I say:
they are harmless, not great.

Their virtue is small.
It does not sing.

It does not risk.
It does not burn.

I do not hate them.
But I do not envy their sleep.

They walk carefully through life -
like men tiptoeing through a dream
they never dared to wake.

They speak of justice,
but only whisper of courage.

They help the weak
not because they are strong,
but because they are afraid
to feel strong themselves.

Their goodness is a habit -
not a choice.

Their hearts beat with the clock,
not the storm.

They have not sinned -
not because they are pure,
but because they have never dared enough
to be tempted.

Their virtue is the shadow
of fear.

I say:
let your virtue be fierce.
Let it have color.
Let it break things.

Be good like a lion -
not like a lamb.

I love the one who makes his own virtue -
who sculpts it from danger,
from laughter,
from solitude.

I love the virtue that has no name
because it must always be reborn."

And Zarathustra turned from the square,
where men handed out medals for politeness,
and walked again into the wind.

Section 6 - On the Rabble

Zarathustra spoke:

"Life is a well
of sweet and bitter water.

And the rabble is a poisoned cup
dipped into it again and again.

I do not hate them -
but I cannot drink with them.

They confuse noise for music,
opinion for thought,
vengeance for justice.

They swarm where greatness stirs -
not to lift it,
but to swarm it to death.

When I give,
they suspect a trap.
When I praise,
they twist it into mockery.

Their joy is not in becoming -
it is in bringing others down
to where becoming cannot happen.

The rabble does not think.
It reacts.

It does not speak.
It repeats.

It does not love.
It devours.

I saw a man of spirit,
once radiant with vision -
until he let the rabble into his ears.
They cheered him,
then chewed him.

And now he smiles with their smile,
speaks with their voice,
walks with their limp.

I say:
build your house on a high rock.
Let no window open to the square.

Do not teach the rabble.
Do not argue with it.
Do not raise it -
walk past it
like a storm past a stagnant pool.

I love the earth.
I love the people -
but not the swarm
that kills thought before it is born."

And Zarathustra turned toward the sea,
where the wind was loud,
but did not lie.

Section 7 - On the Tarantulas

Zarathustra spoke:

"Behold the tarantulas:
they spin webs of justice,
but their poison is vengeance.

In their hearts,
they hate the strong.
They hate joy.
They hate difference.

And so they speak of equality.

But I say to you:
they do not love the equal -
they cannot bear the higher.

Their justice is revenge in disguise.
Their law is bitterness with a mask.

They bite
not because they are wronged,
but because they are small.

The tarantula says:
'All must be equal!'
But what it means is:
'None must rise above me.'

I say:
where true justice grows,
it grows from strength,
not resentment.

Let your heart be a sun,
and your hand a storm -
not a cobweb.

The noble one gives -
not to humble others,
but because he is full.

The tarantula gives only to bind.
Its threads are laws,
spun tight around the rising ones.

And it calls this virtue.

I do not say: kill the tarantulas.
I say: outgrow them.
Leave their webs behind
like old skin.

For the time is coming
when man must choose:
become a flame -
or become a net."

Then Zarathustra crushed a tarantula underfoot and said:

"Look, this was once a teacher of virtue."

Section 8 - On the Famous Wise Men

Zarathustra spoke:

"They sit in high chairs,
these famous wise men.
Their words are deep -
but their roots are shallow.

They speak of truth,
yet fear the sun.

They chew old thoughts
like dry bread,
and call it nourishment.

They do not walk -
they quote.

They do not burn -
they balance.

They wear wisdom like a robe
but do not sweat with life.

I went to them, once.
I listened.
And I heard only echo
wrapped in dignity.

They love moderation,
because they are tired.
They love caution,
because they are afraid.

Their minds are gardens
where nothing wild is allowed to grow.

They praise the past
because it is silent.
They avoid the future
because it sings.

I saw one -
a "sage" -
who smiled with every sentence,
as if every word had already been accepted
by the academy.

But I ask:
where is the philosopher
whose words bleed?

Where is the thinker
who dares a new rhythm?

I do not want carved masks.
I want faces that can still wrinkle with risk.

You call them wise
because they know the names of the stars.
But I say:
the true wise man is one
who builds a star of his own."

Then Zarathustra laughed,
and said to himself:

"Wisdom that does not dance
is not wisdom."

Section 9 - The Night Song

"It is night:
now all the fountains speak louder.

And my soul too
is a fountain.

I sleep not -
I am the fire that watches.

Too long I have burned in solitude.
My silence is heavy with light.

Oh, that I might find someone
who could drink me!

But I live among men
who cannot bear my thirst.

I overflow -
and no cup is deep enough.

I long for companions
who carry lightning in their bones,
who would rather drown in truth
than drift in comfort.

I have given my soul to the wind -
and still, no one comes.

I speak,
but my voice falls
like starlight on closed eyes.

They do not hear my joy.
They do not hear my sorrow.
They do not hear my song.

I am a bell
that has lost its clapper -
I ring only in dreams.

Yet I must sing.
For my soul is a sun
and it cannot sleep.

I sing because I must burn.

I sing because I am alone.

I sing
into the abyss -
and call it friend."

And the night listened.
And the stars
shone back
with silent understanding.

Section 10 - The Dance Song

Zarathustra had been alone in the mountains,
and now he came down to the shore
where the moon hung bright above the sea.

There he saw a young woman dancing -
light as fire,
barefoot on the stone.

And Zarathustra said:

"I am the man who loves dancing.
I am the friend of those who move
like flames.

Let your joy be a storm -
not a sermon.

Let your rhythm be wild,
like the earth in spring.

I do not ask where you learned to dance.
I ask:
What does your body say
when your soul burns?

I once believed in duty.
Now I believe in the circle of the stars.

I once believed in command.
Now I believe in the leap.

You dance,
and I see the truth of the body:

it is not sin -
it is song.

Dance until your fear forgets its name.
Dance until virtue blushes and laughs.

For only in the dance
does man forget the lie of gravity.

I love the dancer
who moves beyond purpose -
who becomes a question
with every step.

I love she who dares the sun
and calls lightning to her heels.

The soul must leap -
or rot."

Then the dancer approached Zarathustra
and whispered:

"I am called Life."

And Zarathustra bowed low -
not in worship,
but in laughter.

Section 11 - The Grave Song

Zarathustra spoke:

“There is a grave inside me -
deep, black, and still.

I buried something there -
a name,
a love,
a former self.

I am not sure what it was.
But it once ruled my heart
like a silent king.

And now, from time to time,
I feel its hand
rise through the soil.

I call it sorrow.
I call it memory.
I call it the shadow of my Yes.

We all bury things.
The question is -
can we sing above them?

I do not dig the grave to mourn -
I dig to know what I survived.

That which does not rise with us
 when we dance
 must be left behind.

I do not want to forget.
 I want to transfigure.

Even the dead
 may feed the root
 of the new tree.

And if I must carry a tomb in me,
 then let it be carved
 with laughter.

Let my grief grow fruit.

For the grave is not the end.
 It is the dark note
 in the song of becoming."

And Zarathustra placed his hand upon the earth
and felt it breathe.

Section 12 - On Self-Overcoming

Zarathustra spoke:

“Where I found living things,
there I heard the language of obedience.

Every living being obeys -
a law,
a hunger,
a rhythm.

But who commands?
And what is freedom?

I say to you:
freedom is not disobedience -
it is self-overcoming.

The will to power
is not the will to rule others -
it is the will to rise above yourself.

Your virtue is your law.
But who wrote it?
And can you outgrow it?

You call something good
because it is easy.
But I ask:
does it sharpen you?

The snake must shed its skin.
The tree must break its bark.
The soul must burn its certainties.

You are not yet noble
if you have not bled
for your own becoming.

I say:
let your soul be firewood -
and let your will be the flame.

He who cannot command himself
forever obeys strangers.

And he who never overcomes himself
becomes doctrine -
not dance.

I love him
who dares to cut off his own hand
if it offends his spirit.

I love her
who breaks her own image
when it blocks the mirror of truth.

Self-overcoming
is the path of the creator.

Do not seek power -
become power.

Do not seek law -
become law.

For only those who burn
their own scaffolding
will ever see the stars."

And Zarathustra fell silent -
as if waiting to be overcome
by his own words.

Section 13 - On Those Who Are Sublime

Zarathustra spoke:

"I look at those who are called 'sublime.'
They stand tall -
but they breathe heavily.

Their virtue has lifted them,
but they carry it like a stone.

They climb,
but they do not dance.

They are proud,
but they are not free.

They have not yet learned to laugh.

Their seriousness betrays
a secret longing to be praised.

They hide their hunger in discipline -
but I see it gnawing at their eyes.

They say: ‘I serve truth.’
But they dream of applause.

Their mountain is too narrow
for joy.

I say:
true greatness does not lean forward -
it overflows.

Do not call sublime
the one who stands above others
but fears the abyss within.

I love the one who surpasses himself
not out of duty,
but from delight.

I love the one
who does not bow to virtue,
but gives it wings.

Let your depth be radiant.
Let your seriousness become song.

For even the highest mountain
must greet the sun
with a smile."

And Zarathustra laughed -
not at them,
but above them.

Section 14 - On the Land of Education

Zarathustra spoke:

"I wandered through the land of education -
and saw many cultivated men,
but few growing ones.

Their minds were tidy gardens,
trimmed with care -
but no wild seed dared bloom there.

They knew much.
But their knowing was like furniture -
arranged, displayed, unused.

I heard them speak of freedom.
But their thoughts came
from textbooks,
not from storms.

I asked them:
'What have you unlearned?'
And they looked at me
as if I had broken a rule.

Their virtue was memorized.
Their rebellion was fashionable.
Their questions
already answered by committee.

They did not listen to their blood -
only to their grades.

I saw one man
polishing his diploma
as if it were a mirror.
But he did not dare look into it.

Another hung quotes on his wall
like trophies,
but could not live a single one.

I say:
education is not to inform -
but to ignite.

The mind is not a bucket -
it is a forge.

Do not become a library of facts.
Become a furnace
of transformation.

I love the one
who forgets everything he has learned
when the time comes to create.

For true learning
is not what you keep -
it is what you burn
to become light."

And Zarathustra turned away
from the halls of instruction,
toward the mountain's wild path.

Section 15 - On Immaculate Perception

Zarathustra spoke:

"You call it pure knowledge.
You call it 'immaculate perception.'

But I ask:
Can the eye be clean
if the soul is afraid to touch?

They want to see the world
like a god above it -
cool, distant, untouched.

They say:
'Let us observe, not participate.
Let us study, not love.'

But life is not a specimen.
It is a flame.

And whoever fears being burned
will never know the fire.

I do not trust the thinkers
who wear gloves.
I trust the ones
whose hands are singed.

They wish to look
without being seen.
To know
without being changed.

But every true perception
stains the soul.

You do not find truth
by avoiding it -
you find it by wrestling it
in the mud,
in the dark,
in the self.

The immaculate ones
wish for a god's view -
and become ghosts.

I say:
blessed are the impure,
for they dare to feel.

Blessed are the wounded,
for they have entered the real.

I love the thinker
who breathes in chaos
and exhales clarity.

I love the seer
who does not blink
when the abyss stares back."

And Zarathustra smeared dust upon his brow
and smiled.

Section 16 - On Scholars

Zarathustra spoke:

"I have seen them -
the scholars.

Bent over books,
their backs curled like question marks.

They sniff out facts
like truffle pigs -
proud of each discovery,
yet never tasting the earth.

They collect knowledge
the way misers hoard coins -
stacking, counting, never spending.

I do not scorn them.
They are useful.
But they are not creators.

They clean the glass
but never look through it.

They polish old thoughts
until they gleam -
then mistake the gleam for light.

The scholar is like a clockmaker:
precise, cautious, mechanical.
But give him a storm -
and he shatters.

They know the roots of words
but not their fire.

They fear the poet,
for he walks beyond their lines.
They fear the philosopher,
for he burns the maps they draw.

They call it objectivity -
but I see fear in their eyes.

I say:
Let knowledge serve becoming.
Let learning be wind,
not walls.

I love the one
who reads until the words dissolve -
and then writes the world anew.

For wisdom is not a cabinet.
It is a flame."

And Zarathustra turned from the library
and walked toward the sea.

Section 17 - On Poets

Zarathustra spoke:

"Since I knew the body,
the spirit has become more spirit to me.

And all that was once poet's lie -
I now see as the fear to name what burns.

Poets lie too much.
They know too little.
They sing of what they do not dare to live.

Their hearts tremble before chaos,
so they wrap it in meter
and call it myth.

They paint the sky
while turning from the earth.

They speak of gods -
but never walk among men.

I say:
let the poet descend!

Let him stain his hands,
break his voice,
and kiss the fire.

The poet must not decorate truth -
he must bleed it.

I have seen poets
who fell in love with their sorrow -
who caressed pain
and never overcame it.

Their words were narcotics -
beautiful,
but dulling the will.

I love the poet
whose verse is a sword -
whose rhyme cuts falsehood open.

I love the one
who shouts his joy
louder than his grief.

For poetry is not escape -
it is confrontation.

Not a mask -
but a mirror,
held to becoming."

And Zarathustra drew a circle in the dirt
and whispered:

"Truth dances best without costume."

Section 18 - On Great Events

Zarathustra spoke:

"There are men
who shout 'history!'
every time the wind blows a different way.

But I ask:
was it great -
or was it only loud?

The crowd loves explosion.
The thinker loves the echo.

I saw a shipwreck once.
Men called it a great event.
But the ship had been rotting for years -
the wreck was just a headline.

The true turning of the earth
happens in silence.

The seed breaks in darkness.
The soul turns in solitude.
The highest peaks
rise without applause.

You say a war changed the world.
I say: the world was already changing -
the war only announced it.

Do not confuse the trumpet
with the triumph.

I say:
greatness is not the flash -
it is the depth that holds
after the light has gone.

And beware the 'great men'
who march to drums -

for many have conquered
only to hide their fear
of being forgotten.

The deepest revolutions
come from those
who have already overcome themselves.

I love the one
whose fire is hidden -
until the forest is already burning.

I love the one
who creates silently -
then walks away
before the statues rise."

And Zarathustra pointed not to the battlefield,
but to the child
learning to walk alone.

Section 19 - The Soothsayer

Zarathustra spoke:

"Once, in a dead city,
I met a man who stared into the dust
and called it prophecy.

He said:
'All is empty.
The world is ash.
The future is void.'

His face was pale
like a candle long burned.

And his words
were colder than the grave.

He claimed to see what was coming -
but what he saw
was only the shadow of his own despair.

He called his sickness: knowledge.
He called his collapse: clarity.

I listened,
and a great silence opened in me.

And in that silence,
I heard a deeper voice say:
Beware the prophet
who preaches paralysis.

For I say to you:
there is no fate
that is not also a door.

There is no truth
that does not demand a new step.

The soothsayer saw only the end -
because he feared the beginning.

He saw night forever -
because he had no dawn within him.

I do not despise him.
I pity him.

But I do not believe him.

I believe in the morning.

I believe in the builder
who raises houses
while the prophet counts rubble.

I believe in the one
who sees what is dying -
and still plants.

I love the one
who dreams despite the silence,
who laughs
while the ground still shakes."

And Zarathustra laid his hand
on the ruined stone
and whispered:

"This too can become a garden."

Section 20 - On Redemption

Zarathustra spoke:

"To redeem the past -
that is what the river of life desires.

Not to erase it.
Not to deny it.
But to transform it.

All 'it was' - that stings!

The bite of the past poisons the spirit
when it cannot be changed.

That is why the spirit of revenge was born.

Revenge is the will's helplessness
before what has already happened.

The bite says:
'It should not have been.'
The venom says:

'I will strike back -
even if it destroys me.'

But I say to you:
Only the creative will redeems.

Only he who says Yes to all that was
has overcome time.

I do not want followers
who carry grudges like shields.

I want creators -
those who turn scars
into stars.

Your enemy is not the pain.
It is your longing
to undo the past
instead of reworking it.

The spirit that overcomes
must not curse -
it must shape.

To redeem what was
is to will it again.

That is the path to freedom."

And Zarathustra looked upon the setting sun and said:

"You do not avenge the night -
you shine through it."

Section 21 - On the Human Image and the Image-Maker

Zarathustra spoke:

"You may wear a face -
but who carved it?

You may walk upright -
but on whose path?

I see many human images,
but few image-makers.

The crowd borrows itself.
It copies the copies.

Each wears the mask of another -
afraid to be unfinished.

But I say:
Be your own sculptor.
Chip away the foreign.
Shape the rough stone.

And if you must crack -
crack boldly.

For only that which is broken
may be remade as whole.

Your face is not yours
until your soul has struck it
like lightning.

And your law is not yours
until your will has burned it
into your bones.

Beware the human image
made by fear.
Beware the virtue
made by obedience.

I love the one
who is still clay -
who has not hardened too soon.

I love the one
who smashes the mirror
and still sees.

For to be human
is not to inherit -
it is to become.

And to become
is to create."

Then Zarathustra passed a statue
and whispered:

"Better rubble from your own hand
than a masterpiece in chains."

Section 22 - On the Great Longing

Zarathustra spoke:

"There is a longing in me
greater than speech.

It rises in the night
like a tide of fire -
not for things,
not for people,
but for becoming.

I do not long to return.
I do not long to arrive.
I long to overflow.

A voice stirs deep in the marrow,
calling not for comfort
but for the dance
that breaks the ground.

I am not sick -
 I am bursting.

I am not empty -
 I am seeking space to pour.

My joy seeks form.
 My soul seeks flame.

I must find a vessel
 worthy of this pressure -
 or I will shatter stone with silence.

This is not a hunger for answers.
 It is the hunger to create.

I do not cry out
 because I lack.
 I cry out
 because I am full.

Do not mistake my longing
 for sorrow.

It is the wind
 that bends the tree
 before it blossoms.

It is the quake
 before the mountain rises.

I love this pain -
 for it births stars.

I love this weight -
 for it is the promise
 of flight."

And Zarathustra lifted his arms
 to the sky of no god
 and said:

"You silence above me -
 you are the womb
 of my thunder."

Book III

Section 1 - The Wanderer

Zarathustra spoke:

"I walk alone.
But I carry many within me.

My shadow has grown long -
for the sun has stayed behind.

I climbed higher to find clarity,
but the air grew thin,
and the silence louder.

I met no man -
only wind,
and the whisper of wings.

But I am not lonely.
I am becoming wide.

For I am no longer only Zarathustra -
I am also his echo,
his wound,
his work.

The path taught me this:
he who goes far
must carry himself as stranger.

And what is strange
is often called mad.

The people once cheered my voice -
now they flee my silence.

They wanted wisdom
as a feast.
But I brought them
the fire that cooks it.

I do not walk toward answers.
I walk toward the source
of my overflowing.

My steps are not progress -
they are pressure
seeking form.

And if I seem distant,
it is because I am standing
inside the horizon.

The mountain does not descend -
the eyes must rise.

I love the one
who loses his way
because the old maps
could not contain him."

And Zarathustra leaned upon his staff,
not from weakness -
but from the weight
of his seeing.

Section 2 - The Vision and the Riddle

Zarathustra spoke:

> "I climbed alone today,
> higher than ever -
> past the snow,
> into the silence
> where only my breath answered me.
>
> And there,
> I saw a door.
>
> Above it was written:
> 'This is the way to eternity.'
>
> But a dog slept across its threshold.
> And I heard no voice.
>
> Then came the vision.
>
> I saw a shepherd choking -
> something dark in his throat,
> coiled, resisting.

He bit -
clenched his teeth -
and ripped out a black snake.

He spat it far.
Then he laughed.

He laughed as no man had ever laughed -
as if the whole earth had cracked
and joy had poured out.

I woke trembling.

And I asked myself:
What did I see?
What did I hear?

Was it a parable?
Was it madness?

Or was it a riddle I must now solve
with my very being?

What is the snake?
What is the laugh?

And what must be bitten through
before joy is born?"

And Zarathustra said nothing more.
But the silence afterward

felt like thunder
still waiting to strike.

Section 3 - On Ecstasy

Zarathustra spoke:

> "I walked through the morning
> drunk with silence.
>
> My limbs moved -
> but I no longer felt the weight of flesh.
>
> I was lifted,
> not by wings,
> but by the fire of inward light.
>
> I passed through the air
> like a note from an unseen string.
>
> The trees bowed.
> The stones pulsed.
> Even my shadow danced ahead of me.
>
> What was this?
> Not madness -
> but ecstasy.

I had burst the skin of myself
and flowed into the world.

The boundaries of 'I'
no longer held.

Was I becoming god?
Or was I finally becoming
completely human?

I looked at a stream
and saw my thought ripple through it.

I touched a leaf
and it sang.

No command.
No need.
Just being that overflows.

And when I returned to myself,
I wept.

Not from sadness -
but from joy too large
for the vessel of the heart.

This is why the gods die -
for joy must be reborn
in the mortal."

And Zarathustra smiled at the mountain wind
as if it were a friend
he had once been.

Section 4 - Before Sunrise

Zarathustra spoke:

"The world slept,
and I watched.

The stars still hung -
shy torches in the deep.

I stood before the dawn,
and I whispered to the night:
Teach me what remains
when all light has yet to come.

Then a voice stirred in me -
not mine,
and yet more mine
than any thought I had ever owned.

It said:
'You are not born of light.
You are born of hunger
for it.

Your soul is not sun -
it is longing for morning.'

And I knew then:
every value I had once praised
was still shadow-bound.

My truth was twilight.
My love - half-lit.
My freedom - still drawn with the ink of night.

The spirit must not only awaken -
it must surpass the sun.

Not worship light -
but create it.

Not await truth -
but shape it as flame.

For what is the dawn
but the courage
to burn through silence?

I do not wait for the sun.
I will it.

I love the one
who stands before sunrise

and says:
'Let there be day!'"

And Zarathustra stretched out his arms
into the cold air
as if he were kindling
a new sky.

Section 5 - On the Virtue That Gives Itself

Zarathustra spoke:

"I do not speak of reward.
I do not speak of punishment.
I speak of the virtue that gives itself away.

Like the tree,
heavy with fruit,
bending downward
not from duty -
but from overflow.

There is a virtue that waits to be praised.
And there is a virtue
that does not wait -
because it does not know
it is virtue.

This one gives -
not from lack,
but from richness.

She laughs when called good.
She shrugs when forgotten.
She gives like the spring
gives green to the mountain.

I do not love your virtue
that calculates and tallies.
That demands thanks
or fears judgment.

That is not virtue -
it is commerce.

I love the virtue
that forgets itself.

The one that dances
after giving
and never looks back.

You say: 'But who will protect such a soul?'
And I say:
Only the strong can afford to be generous.

For giving that is pure
must not come from need -
but from joy.

Blessed is she
whose hand overflows
even when no one sees."

And Zarathustra dropped a flower
into the path of a stranger
and walked on.

Section 6 - On Old and New Tablets

Zarathustra descended from the heights
and carved these words
into the stone of becoming:

"Once, we were given tablets
from on high -
Thou shalt was etched in thunder.

But I say unto you:
Break the old tablets!
The mountain no longer speaks in commands.

You are not here to obey.
You are here to create.

The old virtue spoke:
'Sacrifice yourself!'
The new virtue says:
Give yourself joyfully!

The old law said:
'Thou shalt not lie.'
I say:
Create truth!
And let it dance.

The old virtue wore a mask -
pale, obedient, bowed.

The new virtue stands upright -
with fire in the veins
and laughter in the chest.

What is good?
All that heightens the feeling of power.

What is evil?
All that springs from weakness
and calls it morality.

Let your law be born from your strength.
Not from the fear of falling.

Do not seek reward.
Be the reward.

Do not pray.
Breathe deeply.
Then act.

Let your life be your answer -
not your apology.

The weak speak often of justice -
because they cannot create order.

The brave speak in acts -
because they have no need to beg.

And beware!
Even the conscience can become a tyrant.

Ask not what is permitted.
Ask what you can bear.

I do not write commandments -
I write songs
for those who build.

Let the hammer speak
where the priest once muttered.

Let your tablets crack
if they cannot hold your flame."

And Zarathustra turned his back on the lawgivers
and walked into the wind,
carving only with his footsteps.

Section 7 - The Face and the Riddle

Zarathustra spoke:

"Hear now the riddle
that still burns in me -
for my dream has not loosened its grip.

I saw a coiled path upon a mountain,
and two figures walked it.

One was a child -
golden, laughing, barefoot.
The other: a shadow
heavy with silence.

They walked in circles
yet claimed to move forward.

And from the summit
there came a voice,
as if the mountain itself were speaking:

'All things return.
All paths curve back.

There is no straight line
but the spiral of becoming.'

And I felt myself fall -
not down,
but inward.

Into the very heart of the riddle.

I saw a gateway
where two roads met,
one forward,
one back -
but both led through the same door.

Above it was written:
"Moment."

And as I stood there,
a voice asked me:

"Do you want this again?
And again?
And again -
just as it was,
with no change,
no end,
no escape?"

I could not answer.
My mouth was stone.

And the child looked up at me and laughed.

Not mockery -
but the joy of one
who had already said Yes.

And I awoke,
full of heat
and horror
and wonder."

Zarathustra paused and said:

"This is my deepest riddle:
Would you will your life
exactly as it was -
forever?"

Section 8 - On Redemption

Zarathustra spoke:

"There is a burden that grows heavier
with every step into the past -
the burden of what cannot be undone.

The wound that festers
is not the wound itself,
but the memory
that will not let it close.

Thus was born the cry:
'It should not have been!'

And in that cry -
the poison called revenge.

Revenge is the will's rebellion
against time.
It strikes backward -
but wounds the one who swings.

And so I say:
There is no redemption
in regret.

The past cannot be changed.
But it can be redeemed.

And how?

By willing it again.

By saying to the darkest hour:
"You are mine.

I do not curse you.
I carry you forward."

For the one who can say Yes
to everything that was
is the one who has overcome time.

Do not forgive the past -
transfigure it.

Do not flee your chains -
melt them into tools.

Do not erase -
create deeper.

To redeem is to sing
the wound into beauty.

And the one who learns this -
learns the secret of eternity."

Zarathustra turned his face toward the dusk and said:

"You, who would avenge -
you must first become a redeemer."

Section 9 - On Human Greatness

Zarathustra spoke:

"I do not ask whether you are good.
I ask whether you are growing.

I do not care for your obedience,
your morals,
your trophies.

I ask:
What pressure have you endured?
What flame have you shaped into form?

Greatness is not height.
It is depth.

It is not in shining.
It is in bearing.

To be great
is to stand at the edge of yourself -
without flinching.

To feel the pull of collapse -
and still
choose to build.

I love the one
who knows his weakness
and chooses still
to carry weight.

Who does not hide in humility,
but dares
to speak with thunder.

Who can say Yes to the abyss
and still
plant seeds on its edge.

There are many tall men
who never stood up once.

And many small ones
who have lifted mountains.

I do not ask your measure.
I ask your movement."

And Zarathustra drew a line in the dust
and stepped over it,
as if to say:
Now. Begin.

Section 10 - The Convalescent

Zarathustra lay still for seven days.
He neither ate nor spoke.
His eyes were open -
but saw nothing of this world.

Then he stirred, and spoke:

"It was a sickness, yes -
but not of the body.

I swallowed a thought
too vast,
too heavy.

It burned through me
like fire through dry roots.

I had looked into the deepest abyss:
the eternal return.

Not as a riddle -
but as law.

All things come again.
Not just once,
but forever.

This life.
This pain.
This breath.
This step.

Again.
And again.
And again.

Would you curse it?

Then you are not yet free.

Would you flee it?

Then you are not yet whole.

Would you bless it?

Then - only then -
are you healed.

I lay in the dark
with this knowledge pressing on me
like the weight of all time.

But I rose.

Not because it passed -
but because I embraced it.

I say to you:
To will the eternal return
is to make peace
not with time -
but with being.

He who is healed
does not seek change -
he sings again."

And Zarathustra stood
with the sun behind him
and cast no shadow.

Section 11 - The Other Dance-Song

Zarathustra had wandered long,
and the silence of the mountains
had become his second skin.

But now,
he heard a rhythm - not his own.
A pulse - distant, alive.

He came upon a clearing,
and there stood Life,
again clothed in fire,
again barefoot before the abyss.

And Life said:

"Why do you always climb alone,
you who once danced with me?"

Zarathustra answered:

"I was searching for the Yes
that does not need a partner.
I wanted my joy

to be round enough
to return on its own."

Life laughed.

"You do not become whole
by breaking into pieces."

Then she spun toward him,
a spiral of flame and breath.

"You speak of eternity -
but forget the circle begins
with two."

Zarathustra watched her.
His silence ripened
like fruit in sun.

Then he stepped forward -
not as master,
not as servant,
but as rhythm made flesh.

They danced.

Not to escape.
Not to possess.
But to echo what burns
without consuming.

The earth spun beneath them.
The stars tilted their ears.
And the abyss leaned close,
craving its name.

When the music stilled,
Zarathustra whispered:

"I am not yours, Life.
But I am no longer only mine."

And Life replied:

"This is what it means
to affirm the eternal."

Then she vanished -
as all true partners do -
leaving only dust
and the echo of the dance.

Section 12 - The Other Dance-Song

Zarathustra spoke:

> "Once I loved life
> like a youth loves a flame -
> wildly, blindly, without rhythm.

But now I love her
like a dancer loves the ground -
because it lets him leap.

My joy no longer shouts.
It steps.
It sways.
It enters like music
through the soles of my feet.

I do not want to possess life -
I want to move with her.

I do not command.
I follow the beat
she hides in stone and blood.

She whispers to me:
'Dance, Zarathustra.
Dance beyond fear.
Dance your Yes
into the bones of the earth.'

And I answer with motion.

My philosophy is not a doctrine.
It is a rhythm.

My truth is not shouted.
It is sung

through every limb
in motion.

I trust what dances.
I doubt what kneels.

For I have learned:
only what dances
is still alive.

And what does not dance -
is waiting to be reborn."

And Zarathustra turned
and his shadow did not follow,
for it too had begun to sway.

Section 13 - The Seal

Zarathustra spoke:

"Was it you, little fox,
who whispered in my ear?

You said:
'All things recur.
All joy wants itself again.
Every ring completes its longing
by circling once more.'

And I -
I listened.

My ear heard
what my soul had feared:
that every flame must return,
every wound reopen,
every laughter echo forever.

You asked:
'Zarathustra, do you desire this again -
and again -
and again?'

And I did not flee.
I did not break.
I sealed it with my blood.

I said Yes.

Yes, once more.
Yes, always.
Yes, even to the deepest pain.

For in this Yes,
I became myself.

In this Yes,
I gave form to the formless.

In this Yes,
I became worthy of eternity.

Joy is not fleeting -
it is faithful.

It wants to return.
It wants to remain.

And I am the one
who lets it."

Then Zarathustra pressed his hand to the earth
and whispered:

"Yes. Once more."

Book IV

Section 1 - The Honey Offering

Zarathustra spoke:

"I have grown weary
of giving honey to those
who only want salt.

I brought gifts -
sweet, golden, overflowing -
but they fed their bitterness with it.

My wisdom fermented.
My joy thickened into song.
My solitude became sweet
as wild honey.

And I offered it.

But they spit it out -
or tried to sell it.

I do not blame them.
Their tongues have only tasted
vinegar and revenge.

They crave law,
not laughter.

They want commandments,
not song.

So now I walk again
into my mountain -
with jars of honey sealed,
and joy hidden in silence.

I am not bitter.
I am full.

Let those who hunger
climb high.
Let them arrive empty.

Then I will open
what ferments in me still."

And Zarathustra placed his honey jars
deep into the cave
where only echoes
could reach them.

Section 2 - The Cry of the Disciples

Zarathustra heard a distant noise -
a cry not of joy,
but of desperation.

It was his disciples, shouting:

"Zarathustra!
Where have you gone?

You vanished like the sun
and left us to the night!

We wandered without you -
through dust and doctrine.

And now the world laughs at us.
They call us mad.

They say: 'Zarathustra is dead!'
Or worse: 'He never was.'

But we know you live,
for we still burn
from your fire.

Return!
Speak again!
Give us your voice!"

But Zarathustra stood behind a rock,
listening -
and said nothing.

Then he whispered:

"They do not seek me -
they seek comfort.

They do not want my fire -
they want warmth.

They do not want the path -
they want the echo.

They cry not because they miss truth -
but because their vanity feels abandoned.

Let them learn the silence.
Let them carry their own flame.

Only then
will they be worthy
to hear me again."

And Zarathustra turned
and walked deeper into the mountains.

Section 3 - The Return

Zarathustra walked again among men -
but no one knew him.

They passed him like wind over stone,
as if he were a stranger

or a shadow
of something forgotten.

He smiled, and thought:

"This is the joy of return -
to arrive unknown.

They remember my words,
but not my face.

They quote me
and misunderstand.

They build shrines
to what I have already burned.

Let them.
The mask is my friend.

For only those who see without names,
without need,
without fear -
will know me.

The others see a prophet,
or a madman,
or a myth.

But I -
I am not to be followed.

I am to be heard,
and then left behind."

And a child approached him and said:

"You smell like thunder."

Zarathustra laughed
and gave the child a stone
in the shape of a ring.

Section 4 - On the Ugliest Man

Zarathustra came upon a crooked figure
sitting alone beside a dry well.
The man's face was twisted - not by birth,
but by centuries of guilt,
self-hatred,
and silence.

Zarathustra asked,

"Who are you,
who casts no shadow even at noon?"

The man replied:

"I am the one who killed God.

Not out of hatred,
but because I could no longer bear
His watching.

His gaze burned me.
His silence accused me.
His presence made me
hate myself.

So I buried Him -
beneath the stones
of reason,
science,
and shame.

But now I am the loneliest.

I carry His corpse
in my memory
and in my hunger.

I destroyed the witness -
but not the wound."

Zarathustra sat beside him
and said nothing.

Then he whispered:

"You are not the ugliest
because you killed God.

You are the ugliest
because you have not yet learned
to dance without Him."

And the man wept,
but the tears were dry.

Section 5 - The Beggar's Song

Zarathustra heard music -
not from a lyre,
but from a throat hoarse with hunger.

A beggar sat beside the road,
singing to no one,
eyes closed,
body trembling.

He sang:

"I have nothing.
Not because I lost it -
but because I gave it away.

My riches were too heavy.
They made me deaf
to the whisper of the wind.

So I threw them
into the abyss
and listened.

Now I hear everything.

The ants in the dust.
The sigh of the stone.
The silence of the sun.

I do not need bread -
I need sky.

I do not need shelter -
I need stars.

I do not need pity -
I need ears
to hear my song
without sorrow.

For I am not poor -
I am empty.

And in this emptiness
I overflow."

Zarathustra sat and listened.
Then he placed a stone before the beggar
and said:

> "Here -
> not alms,
> but a weight,
> to keep your song from drifting
> into heaven too soon."

Section 6 - The Shadow-Dance

As the sun set,
Zarathustra noticed a figure
moving just behind him -
not quite his shadow,
but something that moved as he moved,
but not when he stopped.

It danced.

Zarathustra asked:

> "Who are you -
> who follows not my step,
> but my rhythm?"

The shadow replied:

"I am what you cast
when you shine.

I am the echo
of all you deny.

I am your past,
dressed in your posture.

You walk forward -
but I move behind you,
bending light
into memory.

You left me
when you climbed higher.

But I waited -
and learned your dance.

Now, I want to be seen.
Now, I want to be whole."

Zarathustra watched his own silhouette
begin to move
without him.

And he said:

"Then we must dance together -
not one before,
and one behind.

Not master and shadow,
but partners
in the twilight."

And they danced
until the mountain turned blue
and the stars forgot
who cast what light.

Section 7 - The Awakening

Zarathustra slept beneath a tree.
His dreams were deep -
but not silent.

He heard voices:
his past selves,
his disciples,
his doubts.
All speaking,
all circling.

Suddenly he awoke -
not as one disturbed,
but as one called.

He opened his eyes to the stars
and said:

> "This is not the sleep of rest.
> This is the sleep
> before birth.
>
> I dreamed my masks.
> I dreamed my enemies.
> I dreamed my own voice
> turned strange.
>
> But now -
> I wake to myself.
>
> The day does not return
> by force.
> It returns
> because I will it.
>
> I no longer rise
> because of duty
> or hope.
>
> I rise because
> I burn.

I rise because
I must speak again.

My silence has fermented.
My strength has ripened.
My Yes is ready."

He stood and stretched -
not like a man,
but like a bow
drawing itself back
toward song.

Section 8 - The Feast

Zarathustra descended from the mountain
and found a clearing lit by torches.
There stood a long table
set not by gods,
but by seekers -
those who had followed echoes of his words.

Each guest was strange,
wounded,
hungry for something not named.

Zarathustra looked at them and said:

"So -
you have come.

You who wept in riddles,
who cursed me in your sleep,
who dressed in shadows
hoping I would see you.

Now you sit
waiting to be fed."

And they answered:

"We are the higher men -
but we do not feel high.

We climbed ideas
but found no air.

We chased power,
truth,
beauty -
but each turned its back
when touched.

We came not for answers -
but for a flame
that does not consume."

Zarathustra poured wine
and said:

"This feast is not of answers.
It is of hunger.

You are not here to be filled.
You are here to learn
to hunger differently.

To desire
what makes you greater,
not safe."

Then he lifted his cup
and said:

"To the abyss -
and to those
who build bridges across it."

And they drank,
not to forget -
but to remember more sharply.

Section 9 - The Ass Festival

Night deepened.
The torches smoked.
The "higher men" grew restless.

Suddenly, one cried out:

> "Let us give thanks!
> Let us worship!
> Let us adore something greater than
> ourselves!"

And in their hunger to bow,
they crowned an ass -
a simple, bleating beast -
and knelt before it.

They sang:

> "Holy is the burden-bearer!
> Holy is the humble!
> Holy is the one who says Yes
> to everything -
> without thought,
> without pride,
> without question!"

The ass brayed.

Zarathustra stood at the edge of the circle,
silent.

Then he said:

> "You could not bear my flame.
> So you lit a candle
> beneath a beast.
>
> You could not carry the weight of freedom.
> So you returned
> to worship.
>
> You do not want gods -
> you want masters.
>
> You do not want creators -
> you want commandments."

The higher men looked up, ashamed.

Zarathustra continued:

> "You bow not from reverence -
> but from fear.
>
> You seek not meaning -
> but obedience.
>
> You want the world to kneel with you
> so you need not rise."

And then he laughed.
Not in cruelty,
but in clarity.

Section 10 - The Song of Melancholy

After the absurd feast,
after the ass had brayed,
silence fell -
not of peace,
but of sorrow.

Then a voice rose, low and broken,
singing:

> "All things fall.
>
> The stars,
> the hearts,
> the hopes of men.
>
> Even joy decays,
> even song fades,
> even the fire forgets
> why it burned.
>
> I have danced -
> but now I drag my feet.

I have soared -
 but now the sky is mute.

O life,
 why do you bloom
 if only to wilt?

Why do you shine
 if only to blind?

My soul is a harp
 strung too tight.

One more note -
 and it will snap."

Zarathustra listened
 and felt the echo within him.

Then he spoke:

"Yes - melancholy sings true.

But it is not the last song.

You mourn because you have touched
 the beauty of what ends.

But the ending
 is not betrayal -
 it is the rhythm.

Learn to love the fading,
the crack,
the fall.

Only then
can your Yes reach
the depth of things."

And the harp
did not break.
It hummed.

Section 11 - On the Higher Men

Zarathustra stood before them -
the beggar, the shadow, the prophet, the skeptic, the broken lover,
the wise coward, the proud magician -
each calling himself one of the "higher men."

He looked at them long
and said:

"You came for fire -
and I gave you mirrors.

You asked for crowns -
and I showed you your knees.

You speak of spirit -
but you have not breathed.

You wear the mask of wisdom -
but hide behind fear.

You are not higher men -
you are unfinished men.

You climbed mountains
not to look beyond,
but to look down.

You wanted to be different -
not to become more.

You fed on my words -
but spat out my silence.

You quoted my 'Yes' -
but never faced your own abyss."

They lowered their eyes.

Zarathustra stepped closer:

"The higher man does not need to be called so.
He acts.

He sings even when alone.
He laughs even at his fall.

He dies even his own death -
not one borrowed from a god."

And then softly:

"Leave me.

Or rise.

But do not wait for me
to lift you."

Section 12 - The Magician

Zarathustra heard weeping -
but theatrical,
exaggerated,
almost musical.

He found a man in rich robes
collapsing, rising,
sobbing, smiling -
a magician of emotion.

The man cried:

"I suffer the deepest wound!
My soul is torn!
My love is too great for this world!

Am I not noble?
Am I not tragic?
Feel how I feel!
Watch how I fall!"

Zarathustra stood silently.

The magician paused,
then asked:

"Do you not weep with me?"

Zarathustra replied:

"No.

Your sorrow has mirrors,
not roots.

Your pain is performance.
You suffer not to change -
but to be seen.

You do not feel too much.
You display too much.

You do not need comfort -
you need silence."

The magician tried to smile
through tears
but it stuck.

Then Zarathustra said, gently:

> "There is truth in your sorrow -
> but it is buried beneath
> your stage."

Section 13 - The Voluntary Beggar

Zarathustra met a man clothed in rags,
but clean,
measured,
dignified.

The man said:

> "I gave away everything.
> Not because I was forced -
> but because I was full.
>
> I rejected riches,
> not out of hatred -
> but out of love for the simple.

I left my house,
my name,
my books.

Now I live with animals.
They do not ask questions.
They do not flatter.

I eat little.
I sleep under stars.
I am free."

Zarathustra looked at him and replied:

"You have cast off much -
but have you cast off
the one who needs to cast off?

Your simplicity still smells
of pride.

You abandoned your house -
but built a temple in its place.

You say you are free -
but you still flee."

The beggar was silent.

Then Zarathustra said:

"True renunciation does not parade.
It walks invisibly.

It forgets even that it renounced."

Section 14 - The Shadow

Zarathustra was walking alone
when his shadow appeared beside him again -
not dancing this time,
but following heavily,
as if resentful.

The shadow said:

"I have followed you through silence,
through song,
through storm.

I have clung to your feet
while you soared.

And still, you leave me behind.

You seek light -
but I am your depth.

You speak of overcoming -
but I am what you always leave
unspoken."

Zarathustra paused.

"You are not my enemy," he said,
"but you are not yet my friend.

You are what I have not yet
learned to love.

You are memory.
You are guilt.
You are all I could not carry
into the fire."

The shadow whispered:

"Then burn me,
or bind me.

But do not forget me."

And Zarathustra answered:

"I do not forget.
I become."

Section 15 - At Early Dawn

Zarathustra sat alone
as the horizon shifted
from black to silver.

He watched the light approach -
not suddenly,
but like a secret
returning home.

He whispered:

"The night has not lied -
it has listened.

The stars judged nothing.

The darkness asked nothing.

But now comes the dawn -
and it brings
questions."

He felt the wind before he saw the sun.

He said:

"I am ready.

Not for answers -
but for clarity.

Not for peace -
but for song.

Not for certainty -
but for the risk
of joy."

And as the first light touched his face,
Zarathustra stood -
not taller,
but truer.

Section 16 - The Sign

As the sun rose,
Zarathustra looked to the sky
and asked for nothing.

Then, far off,
he heard the cry of an eagle -
and saw it descending.

In its claws:
a serpent,
coiled but not struggling.

They landed at his feet.

Zarathustra looked at them
and said:

"This is my sign.

The highest bird
and the wisest beast -
not as enemies,
but as one flight.

Pride and depth.
Speed and cunning.
Sky and earth.

The master of height
and the master of beneath -
united.

This is how I must walk.

This is how I must speak.

This is how I must give."

Then Zarathustra turned from the mountain
not as preacher,
not as prophet,
but as whole.

He walked
into the valley

with light behind him -
and silence
that no longer needed to be broken.

Section 17 - The Greeting

As dawn warmed the earth,
Zarathustra walked toward his cave.
But before he reached it,
the "higher men" emerged
to meet him.

They bowed,
awkwardly,
as if unsure what to do
with reverence.

Zarathustra paused.

Then one said:

> "We have listened.
> We have eaten your silence.
> We have suffered your gaze.
>
> Now - may we greet you?"

Zarathustra smiled.

“You greet me
not with trumpets,
but with hesitation.

Good.
You are learning.”

Then another said:

“We do not understand you.”

Zarathustra answered:

“I am not here
to be understood.

I am here
to be overcome.”

The wind stirred the trees,
and even the birds
seemed to pause.

Section 18 - The Last King

Among the “higher men”
one now stepped forward -
a man once crowned,
but now cloaked in plainness.

He said:

“I was once called king.
I ruled not with love,
but with fear wrapped in order.

My people obeyed,
but never sang.

I sat on a throne
and felt the rot beneath it.

One day,
I saw a child laugh in chains -
and I knew
my crown was rust.”

Zarathustra looked into his eyes
and said:

“You have abdicated.
But have you descended?

You gave up power -
but do you now give birth?

A true king is not obeyed -
he is outgrown.”

The man bowed again,
this time with no memory of crowns.

Section 19 - Nausea

Zarathustra withdrew from the feast.
The smoke, the noise, the heavy praise -
it clung to him
like the stench of rot beneath perfume.

He walked alone into the rocks
and spoke aloud:

"I am sick of men.

Their praise stinks of need.
Their love strangles.
Their mouths drip wisdom -
and bite behind the smile.

I have shown them the height -
and they built idols at the base.

I danced -
and they asked for instructions.

I roared -
and they took notes.

I gave wine -
they watered it down
and called it virtue.

This feast is not joy.
It is digestion without fire.

I do not hate them -
I choke on them.

O solitude,
my clean air -
receive me again!"

He dropped to one knee,
not in prayer,
but to vomit up mankind.

Section 20 - The Recovery

Zarathustra lay alone -
empty,
purged,
silent.

No words.
No gods.
No men.

Only the sky above him,
and the slow rhythm
of his own breath.

Then he whispered:

> "I do not return
> because I was wrong.
>
> I return
> because I have more to give.
>
> My Yes is not a reaction -
> it is a source.
>
> My love is not naive -
> it has passed through nausea.
>
> My solitude is not escape -
> it is the hearth
> from which I bake new suns."

He stood,
light,
calm,
quiet.

Then he laughed -
not wildly,
not bitterly -
but like a man who has forgotten to doubt.

He said:

“My sickness has served me.
I have shed imitation
and excreted flattery.

I am not here to teach -
but to overflow.

Whoever drinks - drinks.
Whoever thirsts - will find me.

But I am not waiting.”

And he walked on,
not toward followers,
but toward life itself.

Glossary of Living Terms

(Not for memorizing - only for burning brighter)

Overman (Übermensch)

Not a better human. Not a master race.
The one who overcomes - who becomes more than man by burning through him.
He creates values not from law or fear, but from the sacred Yes of the will.

Eternal Return (Die ewige Wiederkunft)

Not a doctrine. Not a cosmology.
A test: Would you choose this life again - and again - down to every wound?
He who affirms recurrence affirms life without remainder.

Will to Power (Wille zur Macht)

Not domination. Not control.
The force that wants to become more, to shape, to

transform.
Power not over others - but over one's own becoming.

The Last Man (Der letzte Mensch)

He avoids pain. He avoids danger. He avoids greatness.
He says, "We invented happiness."
But he no longer dances. No longer risks. No longer creates.

The Tightrope-Walker

A symbol for man.
Stretched between beast and Overman.
A crossing, not a dwelling. A danger, not a comfort.

Self-Overcoming (Selbstüberwindung)

The act of burning one's own virtues to create new flame.
He who does not overcome himself becomes doctrine.
He who dares becomes song.

God is Dead (Gott ist tot)

Not a claim of atheism.
A diagnosis: the old values are hollow.
Man must become the meaning-maker now - or else fall beneath his own shadow.

Descent (Der Abstieg)

Zarathustra's path downward.
From mountain to market. From silence to speech.
Every descent is a test of giving without being understood.

Yes (Ja)

Not agreement. Not submission.
The deepest affirmation.
The creative response to existence without illusion.

Flame

Nietzsche's true metaphor for spirit.
Burns, transforms, illuminates.
Everything untested by fire remains unformed.

Dance

More than joy. More than motion.
The way spirit becomes body.
Where thought leaps, and gravity loses its grip.

Laughter

Not mockery. Not escape.
The highest expression of strength -
when the abyss is seen, and still we say: Yes.

www.ingramcontent.com/pod-product-compliance
Lightning Source LLC
LaVergne TN
LVHW081324110826
845149LV00007B/1586

9781968044572